I0457224

30-DAY
WOMEN'S
DEVOTIONAL

JOURNAL

"Transparency – Owning Your Impact in Relationships"

INTRODUCTION

What Clarity Looks Like

Clarity doesn't mean you have everything figured out — it means you're willing to be honest about where you are. When we allow God to shine a light on the parts of us that we've hidden or ignored, that's where true healing begins.

Transparency is not weakness; it's the kind of strength that invites growth. It says, "I'm not perfect, but I'm present." Clarity begins when we choose truth over comfort and healing over pride.

This devotional journal was created to help you pause, reflect, and take responsibility for the energy you bring into your relationships — with God, yourself, and others. Over the next 30 days, you'll be guided through Scripture, prayer, reflection, and journaling. Each day offers an opportunity to get real, release what doesn't serve you, and rebuild from a place of peace and purpose.

Remember: **God can't heal what we hide.**

So, let's start this journey with an open heart and a willing spirit.

HOW TO USE THIS JOURNAL

Each day is designed to take about 15–20 minutes of reflection time, though you can go slower if you wish. Some women like to do their devotion first thing in the morning; others prefer evenings when the day has settled.

There is no "right" way — only a **heart willing to listen**.

1.Scripture Focus – Begin by reading the day's verse. Sit with it. Read it aloud. Ask God what He's showing you through these words.

2.Devotional Reflection – Read the short devotional message. These are written to help you see yourself and your relationships in light of God's truth and love.

3.Reflection Prompt / Guided Journaling – Here's where transformation happens. Answer honestly. Write freely — even if your words feel raw. This space is just for you and God.

4.Prayer or Affirmation – End each entry with gratitude or surrender. You may write your own prayer or repeat the one given. Let it anchor your heart.

5.(Optional) Action Step / Accountability Thought – Apply what you've learned that day. These are small but powerful steps toward emotional maturity and spiritual alignment.

WEEK 1

Seeing Yourself Clearly
Psalm 139:23–24

Self-examination, honesty with self and God

THE POWER OF TRUTH

DAY I

- **Scripture:**

"Then you will know the truth, and the truth will set you free."
— John 8:32

- **Reflection:**

Truth is liberating, but it can also be confronting. Many of us struggle with transparency because we fear judgment or rejection. But honesty — especially with ourselves — is the foundation of clarity. The moment we face our truth, we open the door for change. God doesn't work through denial; He works through honesty.

- **Journal Prompts:**

1. Where in your life have you avoided being completely honest, with yourself or someone else?

_____

_____

_____

_____

_____

_____

_____

_____

_____

2.   What would freedom look like if you chose truth over comfort?

_____

_____

_____

_____

_____

_____

_____

_____

_____

_____

_____

- **Prayer:**

Lord, give me the courage to see myself clearly and to speak truth in love. Heal the parts of me that hide out of fear, and help me trust that honesty leads to freedom. Amen.

- **Today's Action:**

Have one honest conversation — even if it's just with yourself in your journal.

HEALING THROUGH FORGIVENESS

- **Scripture:**

"Bear with each other and forgive one another… Forgive as the Lord forgave you." — *Colossians 3:13*

- **Reflection:**

Forgiveness isn't about forgetting what was done; it's about freeing yourself from the weight of what happened. Unforgiveness keeps your heart hostage. The longer you hold on, the heavier it gets. Healing begins the moment you release the need to make someone else pay for your pain.

- **Journal Prompts:**

1.   Who or what do you still need to forgive?

_____

_____

_____

_____

_____

_____

_____

_____

_____

_____

_____

2. What would it take for you to finally let it go?

_____

_____

_____

_____

_____

_____

_____

_____

_____

_____

_____

_____

- **Prayer:**

God, I release the pain that has kept me bound. Help me forgive not because they deserve it, but because I deserve peace. Amen.

- **Today's Action:**

Write a letter of forgiveness — you don't have to send it, but let it set you free.

CHOOSING PEACE OVER CHAOS

DAY 3

- **Scripture:**

"Peace I leave with you; my peace I give you." — John 14:27

- **Reflection:**

Peace isn't passive, it's a choice. We often mistake chaos for normal because we've lived in survival mode for so long. But God calls us to live in peace, not in constant reaction. True peace comes when you stop trying to control everything and start trusting God's order.

- **Journal Prompts:**

1. What situations or people disrupt your peace most often?

_____

_____

_____

_____

_____

_____

_____

_____

_____

_____

2. How can you create more room for peace in your daily life?

_____

_____

_____

_____

_____

_____

_____

_____

_____

_____

- **Prayer:**

Lord, quiet my spirit when life feels loud. Remind me that peace is not the absence of problems, but the presence of You. Amen.

- **Today's Action:**

Take 15 minutes of quiet time today no phone, no music, just stillness.

LETTING GO OF CONTROL

- **Scripture:**

"Trust in the Lord with all your heart and lean not on your own understanding." — Proverbs 3:5

- **Reflection:**

We often try to control every detail because we fear what happens when we don't. But the need for control is usually rooted in fear — fear of being hurt again, fear of failure, or fear of the unknown. God is inviting you to rest, not wrestle. When you let go, you make room for Him to do what only He can do.

- **Journal Prompts:**

1. Where in your life do you struggle to trust God's plan?

_____

_____

_____

_____

_____

_____

_____

_____

2. What would it look like to surrender that situation today?

_____

_____

_____

_____

_____

_____

_____

_____

_____

_____

_____

_____

- **Prayer:**

God, teach me to release my need to control and to trust that Your plans are better than mine. Amen.

- **Today's Action:**

Write down one thing you're afraid to release. Say it out loud and give it to God.

BOUNDARIES ARE HOLY

- **Scripture:**

"Above all else, guard your heart, for everything you do flows from it." — *Proverbs 4:23*

- **Reflection:**

Boundaries don't make you cold — they make you clear. They protect the peace God gave you and help you love others from a healthy place. You can be kind and still say no. You can care deeply and still choose distance. Setting boundaries isn't about rejection; it's about protection.

- **Journal Prompts:**

1. Where do you need to set or reinforce a boundary in your life?

_____

_____

_____

_____

_____

_____

_____

_____

_____

_____

2.   How have unclear boundaries affected your peace?

_____

_____

_____

_____

_____

_____

_____

_____

_____

_____

_____

_____

- **Prayer:**

Lord, help me set boundaries that honor You and protect my peace. Teach me that saying "no" can be an act of obedience. Amen.

- **Today's Action:**

Identify one place you've been overextending yourself and take one small step to reclaim your time or energy.

DAY 6

HEALING TAKES TIME

- **Scripture:**

"He heals the brokenhearted and binds up their wounds." —
Psalm 147:3

- **Reflection:**

Healing isn't a straight line — it's a journey. Some days you'll feel whole; others you'll feel raw. Both are part of the process. God isn't disappointed by your pace; He's patient with your progress. Stop rushing what's meant to grow. Healing is holy work, and it takes time.

- **Journal Prompts:**

1. What area of your life still feels tender or unfinished?

_____

_____

_____

_____

_____

_____

_____

_____

_____

_____

2. What is one small way you can show yourself grace today?

_____

_____

_____

_____

_____

_____

_____

_____

_____

_____

_____

- **Prayer:**

God, remind me that healing is not about perfection, but progress. Help me trust the process and be gentle with myself along the way. Amen.

- **Today's Action:**

Write an encouraging note to yourself as if you were your own best friend.

DAY 7

CONFRONTING FEAR

- **Scripture:**

"For God has not given us a spirit of fear, but of power and love and a sound mind." — 2 Timothy 1:7

- **Reflection:**

Fear thrives in silence. It grows when we don't name it. But once you confront fear with faith, it loses its power. God didn't create you to live small or scared. Courage doesn't mean you're not afraid — it means you choose to move forward anyway.

- **Journal Prompts:**

1. What fear has been holding you back lately?

2.   How would your life change if you faced that fear with faith?

_____

_____

_____

_____

_____

_____

_____

_____

_____

_____

_____

- **Prayer:**

Lord, help me to recognize fear when it shows up and replace it with faith. Amen.

- **Today's Action:**

Take one step today — even a small one — toward something that's been intimidating you.

WEEK 2

Owning Your Words
Proverbs 18:21

The power of speech, tact, and tone

GRATITUDE IN THE GRIND

- **Scripture:**

"Give thanks in all circumstances; for this is God's will for you in Christ Jesus." — 1 Thessalonians 5:18

- **Reflection:**

Life won't always be easy, but gratitude shifts your perspective. When you focus on what's working instead of what's missing, you invite joy into your process. Gratitude doesn't erase struggle; it helps you find beauty within it.

- **Journal Prompts:**

1. What three things can you thank God for today — even in the middle of your challenges?

_____

_____

_____

_____

_____

_____

_____

_____

_____

_____

_____

2.   How does gratitude change the way you see your situation?

_____
_____
_____
_____
_____
_____
_____
_____
_____
_____
_____

- **Prayer:**

God, thank You for being good even when life isn't easy. Help me find gratitude in the grind and contentment in the chaos. Amen.

- **Today's Action:**

List three blessings out loud today. Speak them until they feel real.

WHEN LOVE LOOKS LIKE DISTANCE

- **Scripture:**

"Let your 'Yes' be 'Yes,' and your 'No,' 'No.'" — *Matthew 5:37*

- **Reflection:**

Sometimes love means stepping back. You can still care and choose distance. Every connection doesn't deserve access, and every relationship doesn't require your presence. Healthy love includes space. Let God teach you how to love people without losing yourself.

- **Journal Prompts:**

1. Who or what have you needed to love from a distance?

2. How can you still honor God while protecting your peace?

_____

_____

_____

_____

_____

_____

_____

_____

_____

_____

_____

- **Prayer:**

Lord, teach me to love wisely — with grace, honesty, and boundaries. Amen.

- **Today's Action:**

Spend time praying for someone you've had to distance yourself from — not out of guilt, but love.

OWNING YOUR IMPACT

DAY
10

- **Scripture:**

"Let us not love with words or speech but with actions and in truth." — 1 John 3:18

- **Reflection:**

Transparency isn't just about what we say — it's about how we show up. Your words matter, but your actions define your impact. Every interaction leaves an imprint. The more aware you become of your influence, the more intentional you'll be about leaving people better than you found them.

- **Journal Prompts:**

1. How do you want people to experience you?

2. Where can you take responsibility for how you've shown up in a relationship?

_____

_____

_____

_____

_____

_____

_____

_____

_____

_____

_____

_____

- **Prayer:**

God, help me to live with integrity and kindness. Let my actions reflect Your love and truth. Amen.

- **Today's Action:**

Do one intentional act of kindness today — quietly, without expecting anything in return.

THE POWER OF TRUTH

- **Scripture:**

"Be still before the Lord and wait patiently for him." — *Psalm 37:7*

- **Reflection:**

Waiting seasons are never wasted seasons. God uses them to build patience, strengthen faith, and align timing. But waiting doesn't mean doing nothing — it means trusting while still preparing. Every delay is either divine protection or preparation. The question isn't, "How long must I wait?" but "Who am I becoming while I wait?"

- **Journal Prompts:**

1. What situation in your life feels like it's on hold right now?

2.   How can you use this time to grow instead of grumble?

_____

_____

_____

_____

_____

_____

_____

_____

_____

_____

_____

- **Prayer:**

God, teach me to trust Your timing. Help me rest in knowing that what's for me will not miss me. Amen.

- **Today's Action:**

List three lessons this waiting season has taught you so far.

ACCOUNTABILITY IS LOVE

DAY 12

- **Scripture:**

"Faithful are the wounds of a friend; profuse are the kisses of an enemy." — Proverbs 27:6

- **Reflection:**

True love doesn't avoid hard conversations — it invites them. Accountability is uncomfortable, but it's a form of care. The people who love you enough to challenge you are gifts from God. Growth requires honesty, even when it stings.

- **Journal Prompts:**

1. Who in your life helps hold you accountable — and how do you respond to correction?

2. Where might God be calling you to lovingly hold someone else accountable?

_____

_____

_____

_____

_____

_____

_____

_____

_____

_____

_____

- **Prayer:**

Lord, surround me with people who tell me the truth, not just what I want to hear. Give me humility to receive correction with grace. Amen.

- **Today's Action:**

Reach out to a friend or mentor and thank them for helping you grow in truth.

THE POWER OF TRUTH

- **Scripture:**

"Let the redeemed of the Lord tell their story." — *Psalm 107:2*

- **Reflection:**

Your voice has power — but life's pain can make you quiet. Somewhere along the way, you may have learned to shrink, to avoid conflict, or to keep peace by losing your truth. God didn't give you a voice to silence it; He gave it to heal, to testify, and to speak life.

- **Journal Prompts:**

1. Where have you felt unheard or silenced?

2.   What truth do you need to start speaking again?

_____

_____

_____

_____

_____

_____

_____

_____

_____

_____

_____

- **Prayer:**

God, restore my confidence to speak truth in love. Let my voice reflect healing, not hurt. Amen.

- **Today's Action:**

Write one declaration of truth about yourself and say it aloud today.

THE POWER OF TRUTH

- **Scripture:**

"My grace is sufficient for you, for my power is made perfect in weakness." — 2 Corinthians 12:9

- **Reflection:**

You extend grace to everyone else — but do you offer it to yourself? God's grace doesn't stop where your mistakes begin. He knew your flaws before you did and still called you worthy. Perfection isn't required for purpose. Give yourself permission to be a work in progress.

- **Journal Prompts:**

1. What mistake or regret do you still hold against yourself?

2.   What would it feel like to finally release it?

_____

_____

_____

_____

_____

_____

_____

_____

_____

_____

_____

- **Prayer:**

Lord, remind me that Your grace covers my weakness. Help me stop criticizing what You're still healing. Amen.

- **Today's Action:**

Write down one thing you forgive yourself for — and tear it up as a symbol of release.

WEEK 3

Healing Through Accountability
James 5:16

Owning mistakes and embracing forgiveness

THE COMPANY YOU KEEP

- **Scripture:**

"Do not be misled: 'Bad company corrupts good character.'" —
1 Corinthians 15:33

- **Reflection:**

Your circle shapes your spirit. Some people help you grow, others stunt it. The closer someone is to you, the more influence they have — and not everyone deserves that level of access. Evaluate who feeds your faith and who drains it.

- **Journal Prompts:**

1. Who in your life strengthens your walk with God?

2.   Who or what might you need to create distance from?

_____

_____

_____

_____

_____

_____

_____

_____

_____

_____

_____

- **Prayer:**

God, help me to walk with wise and loving people. Remove connections that distract me from Your purpose. Amen.

- **Today's Action:**

Send a message of gratitude to someone who genuinely pours into your life.

BREAKING CYCLES

- **Scripture:**

"See, I am doing a new thing! Now it springs up; do you not perceive it?" — Isaiah 43:19

- **Reflection:**

You can't heal what you keep repeating. Many of us live inside cycles we didn't create but have the power to end. Whether it's how we love, communicate, or respond to pain — God invites us to break patterns that no longer serve our growth. You are not bound by what you've been through.

- **Journal Prompts:**

1. What cycle in your life or family line needs to stop with you?

_____

_____

_____

_____

_____

_____

_____

_____

_____

_____

2.   What new pattern can you start today?

_____

_____

_____

_____

_____

_____

_____

_____

_____

_____

- **Prayer:**

God, give me the courage to be the first to do it differently. Let generational healing begin with me. Amen.

- **Today's Action:**

Write down one behavior or mindset you will no longer carry forward.

WALKING IN WISDOM

- **Scripture:**

"If any of you lacks wisdom, you should ask God, who gives generously to all without finding fault." — James 1:5

- **Reflection:**

Wisdom isn't just knowledge — it's discernment in action. It's the ability to see beyond emotion and choose what honors God. When you ask Him for wisdom, He gives it — not to make you superior, but to make you stable.

- **Journal Prompts:**

1. In what area of your life do you need divine wisdom right now?

_____

_____

_____

_____

_____

_____

_____

_____

_____

_____

2. How can you slow down to listen before reacting?

_____

_____

_____

_____

_____

_____

_____

_____

_____

_____

_____

- **Prayer:**

Lord, quiet my spirit long enough to hear Your wisdom. Teach me to pause before I respond. Amen.

- **Today's Action:**

Before you make a decision today, take one minute to pray for direction.

VULNERABILITY IS STRENGTH

DAY 18

- **Scripture:**

"Confess your sins to each other and pray for each other so that you may be healed." — James 5:16

- **Reflection:**

The world teaches us to hide our pain; God calls us to share it. Vulnerability isn't weakness — it's bravery wrapped in honesty. When you open up, you create space for connection, compassion, and healing.

- **Journal Prompts:**

1. What part of yourself do you still hide from others?

_____

_____

_____

_____

_____

_____

_____

_____

_____

_____

2.   What would happen if you let someone see that part of you?

_____

_____

_____

_____

_____

_____

_____

_____

_____

_____

_____

_____

- **Prayer:**

God, help me to be courageous in my vulnerability. Let my openness inspire healing in others. Amen.

- **Today's Action:**

Share one honest truth about your heart with someone safe today.

 **DAY 19**

OBEDIENCE OVER OPINION

- **Scripture:**

"Am I now trying to win the approval of human beings, or of God?"
— *Galatians 1:10*

- **Reflection:**

You can't please everyone — and you weren't called to. Obedience to God often means disappointing people. But your purpose can't thrive under the pressure of other people's opinions. Follow what He told you to do, not what they think you should do.

- **Journal Prompts:**

1. Where are you still seeking approval from others more than from God?

2.   What would obedience look like in that area?

_____

_____

_____

_____

_____

_____

_____

_____

_____

_____

_____

_____

- **Prayer:**

Lord, help me choose Your will over others' expectations. Make me confident in Your calling. Amen.

- **Today's Action:**

Take one bold step today that aligns with obedience, not approval.

FAITH IN THE UNKNOWN

- **Scripture:**

"For we walk by faith, not by sight." — *2 Corinthians 5:7*

- **Reflection:**

Faith isn't about certainty — it's about trust. When you can't see the outcome, you lean on the One who can. The unknown can feel intimidating, but it's also where miracles unfold. You don't need all the answers — just one act of trust at a time.

- **Journal Prompts:**

1. What area of your life feels uncertain right now?

_____

_____

_____

_____

_____

_____

_____

_____

_____

_____

2. How can you show faith through action today?

_____

_____

_____

_____

_____

_____

_____

_____

_____

_____

_____

- **Prayer:**

God, even when I don't see it, help me believe You're working. Strengthen my faith in the unseen. Amen.

- **Today's Action:**

Write down one fear about the unknown — then write "God is greater" right beside it.

FAITH OVER FEELINGS

- **Scripture:**

"The heart is deceitful above all things and beyond cure; who can understand it?" — Jeremiah 17:9

- **Reflection:**

Feelings are real but not always reliable. Sometimes our emotions speak louder than truth, convincing us that temporary pain defines permanent reality. Faith anchors us when feelings fluctuate. Trust God even when your emotions don't agree — He remains constant.

- **Journal Prompts:**

1. When have your feelings led you away from your faith?

2. What truth from God's Word can you hold onto when emotions feel overwhelming?

_____

_____

_____

_____

_____

_____

_____

_____

_____

_____

_____

_____

- **Prayer:**

Lord, teach me to trust what You've said more than what I feel. Remind me that faith is greater than emotion. Amen.

- **Today's Action:**

When a strong emotion rises today, pause and pray before reacting.

WEEK 4

Loving Without Losing Yourself
1 Corinthians 13

Setting boundaries, walking in grace

THE GIFT OF STILLNESS

DAY 22

- **Scripture:**

"Be still, and know that I am God." — Psalm 46:10

- **Reflection:**

The world rewards hustle, but God invites stillness. Silence is where you hear His whisper — where He restores what chaos tries to take. When you slow down, you notice His presence in ways you miss when rushing. Stillness is not laziness; it's alignment.

- **Journal Prompts:**

1. What distractions keep you from stillness?

_____

_____

_____

_____

_____

_____

_____

_____

_____

_____

2. How can you create a quiet space to meet with God this week?

_____

_____

_____

_____

_____

_____

_____

_____

_____

_____

_____

- **Prayer:**

God, calm my mind and settle my spirit. Meet me in the quiet moments and remind me that You are enough. Amen.

- **Today's Action:**

Take five minutes today to sit in silence and breathe deeply — no phone, no noise, just you and God.

THE POWER OF PERSPECTIVE

- **Scripture:**

"Do not conform to the pattern of this world, but be transformed by the renewing of your mind." — Romans 12:2

- **Reflection:**

Perspective changes everything. The same situation can feel hopeless or hopeful depending on how you see it. God invites you to see life through His lens — one of purpose, not punishment. When your mind shifts, your reality begins to follow.

- **Journal Prompts:**

1. Where might you need to shift your perspective?

2. What truth has God been trying to show you lately?

_____

_____

_____

_____

_____

_____

_____

_____

_____

_____

_____

- **Prayer:**

Lord, renew my mind. Help me see what You see — even when it doesn't look like what I expected. Amen.

- **Today's Action:**

Write down one thought you want to release and one new truth you want to embrace.

LOVE THAT HEALS

- **Scripture:**

"And above all these put-on love, which binds everything together in perfect harmony." — Colossians 3:14

- **Reflection:**

Love heals — not the kind that ignores pain, but the kind that chooses compassion anyway. God's love isn't earned; it's received. When you start from that truth, it becomes easier to love others from a place of fullness, not emptiness.

- **Journal Prompts:**

1. What would it look like to love from a healed heart instead of a hurt one?

---

2.   Who in your life needs to experience more grace from you?

_____

_____

_____

_____

_____

_____

_____

_____

_____

_____

_____

- **Prayer:**

God, help me to love like You — freely, fully, and without fear.
Heal me so that my love reflects Your heart. Amen.

- **Today's Action:**

Do one kind act today for someone who won't expect it.

RELEASING SHAME

- **Scripture:**

"There is therefore now no condemnation for those who are in Christ Jesus." — Romans 8:1

- **Reflection:**

Shame keeps you stuck in a story God has already rewritten. It whispers that you are what you did — but grace says you are forgiven and free. You can't change your past, but you can let God use it to change you.

- **Journal Prompts:**

1. What old story of shame are you still believing?

2. How would your life feel if you fully accepted God's forgiveness?

_____

_____

_____

_____

_____

_____

_____

_____

_____

_____

_____

- **Prayer:**

Lord, I release the shame that has held me captive. Remind me that Your grace is greater than my guilt. Amen.

- **Today's Action:**

Look at yourself in the mirror today and say, "I am forgiven. I am free."

_____

PROTECTING YOUR PEACE

DAY 26

- **Scripture:**

"The Lord will fight for you; you need only to be still." — *Exodus 14:14*

- **Reflection:**

Peace is sacred — it's not something you beg for; it's something you protect. Sometimes protecting your peace means walking away from conversations that no longer serve your growth. You don't owe access to anyone who keeps you in anxiety.

- **Journal Prompts:**

1. What or who tends to disturb your peace?

_____

_____

_____

_____

_____

_____

_____

_____

_____

2.   What boundaries can you set to protect your emotional space?

- **Prayer:**

God, thank You for peace that surpasses understanding. Help me guard it with wisdom and courage. Amen.

- **Today's Action:**

Say "no" to one thing that drains your peace today.

BECOMING WHOLE

- **Scripture:**

"You will keep in perfect peace those whose minds are steadfast, because they trust in you." — Isaiah 26:3

- **Reflection:**

Wholeness isn't about having it all together — it's about being aligned. When your mind, body, and spirit agree with truth, you become whole. Healing connects the fragmented parts of your story into something meaningful. You are not missing anything — you are becoming.

- **Journal Prompts:**

1. What parts of yourself still feel disconnected?

_____

_____

_____

_____

_____

_____

_____

_____

_____

_____

_____

2. What would "wholeness" look like for you today?

_____

_____

_____

_____

_____

_____

_____

_____

_____

_____

_____

- **Prayer:**

God, make me whole in every area of my life. Align me with Your peace and purpose. Amen.

- **Today's Action:**

Do something today that nourishes your spirit — journaling, resting, or worshiping.

DAY 28 CLARITY THROUGH SURRENDER

- **Scripture:**

"Commit your way to the Lord; trust in him, and he will act." — *Psalm 37:5*

- **Reflection:**

Clarity doesn't come from control — it comes from surrender. The moment you stop trying to figure everything out, you make space for God to reveal the next step. Surrender isn't weakness; it's wisdom. It's saying, "God, You lead, and I'll follow."

- **Journal Prompts:**

1. What situation do you need to surrender today?

2. What would trusting God fully look like for you?

_____

_____

_____

_____

_____

_____

_____

_____

_____

_____

_____

- **Prayer:**

Lord, I release my need to know and control. Lead me in peace and remind me that surrender is strength. Amen.

- **Today's Action:**

Write a prayer of surrender for whatever you've been worrying about.

Day 29-30

Walking in Transparency Daily
Micah 6:8

Living a lifestyle of authenticity and compassion

LIVING TRANSPARENT

- **Scripture:**

"Therefore confess your sins to each other and pray for each other so that you may be healed." — James 5:16

- **Reflection:**

Transparency brings healing. It invites accountability and community. When you stop pretending and start being honest, you allow others to see God's grace through you. Transparency isn't about exposure; it's about freedom.

- **Journal Prompts:**

1. Where are you still wearing a mask?

_____

_____

_____

_____

_____

_____

_____

_____

_____

2. What would authentic living look like for you now?

_____

_____

_____

_____

_____

_____

_____

_____

_____

_____

_____

_____

- **Prayer:**

God, help me live honestly — with You, with myself, and with others. Let my transparency inspire healing around me. Amen.

- **Today's Action:**

Share one truth about your journey with someone you trust.

WALKING IN CLARITY

DAY 30

- **Scripture:**

"Your word is a lamp for my feet, a light on my path." — *Psalm 119:105*

- **Reflection:**

You've spent 30 days looking inward, confronting truth, and choosing healing. Clarity doesn't mean perfection — it means awareness. Now that you see more clearly, it's time to walk in purpose. Keep choosing honesty, forgiveness, and peace. They are the keys to sustaining the clarity you've gained.

- **Journal Prompts:**

1. What are the biggest lessons these 30 days have taught you?

_____

_____

_____

_____

_____

_____

_____

_____

_____

_____

_____

2.   How will you continue to live with clarity from this day forward?

_____
_____
_____
_____
_____
_____
_____
_____
_____
_____
_____
_____

- **Prayer:**

God, thank You for the clarity You've brought into my life. Help me live out what I've learned and keep growing in truth. Amen.

- **Today's Action:**

Write a declaration of clarity — one that begins with "From this day forward..." and keep it somewhere you can see it.

Final Reflection

Living with Clarity

Transparency isn't a moment; it's a lifestyle. Continue
showing up as your whole self — open, aware, and
growing. The more honest you are with God, the clearer
your path becomes.

- **Final Notes:**

_____

_____

_____

_____

_____

_____

_____

_____

_____

_____

_____

www.ingramcontent.com/pod-product-compliance
Lightning Source LLC
Chambersburg PA
CBHW051553120626
46551CB00013B/1495